Dirty Boys: Why Bathe?

Cleaning Ears and Other Parts

A Picture Book for Kids

By Lisa Strattin

© 2013 Lisa Strattin

To see more titles, visit the author's website at

LisaStrattin.com

All information in this book has been carefully researched and checked for factual accuracy. However, the author and publisher makes no warranty, express or implied, that the information contained herein is appropriate for every individual, situation or purpose and assume no responsibility for errors or omissions. The reader assumes the risk and full responsibility for all actions, and the author will not be held responsible for any loss or damage, whether consequential, incidental, special or otherwise that may result from the information presented in this book.

I have relied on my own experiences as well as many different sources for this book and I have done my best to check facts and give credit where it is due. In the event that any material is used without proper permission, please contact me so that the oversight can be corrected.

Table of Contents

3

Why Do Boys Love Getting Dirty?

Where boys are concerned - Is there anything as
much fun as playing in mud?

But the fact is, as much as boys love getting dirty
– it is important to be clean once you finish playing.
When you were little, you always took baths – most of
the time, your mom or dad would help to get you clean –
from your head to your toes.

But now that you are a big boy – you know that a shower is the best way to get clean. This is because you have clean water pouring over you the whole time. This is a much better way to get really clean.

What Parts Should You Clean?

You have a lot of body parts – so here is a picture to show you all of the parts you have. Many of these parts need to be washed every time you get in the shower.

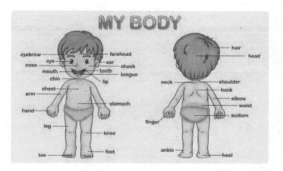

Cleaning Ears

One thing you should know is that the insides of your ears naturally clean themselves. You should give them just a little bit of help on the outside. But never, ever stick anything into your ears. This includes cotton swabs. But you can use these to clean the outer parts of your ears.

Your parents will help you to clean your ears until they feel you are ready to do it on your own. They know to use the cotton swab on the outside of your ears and not the inside!

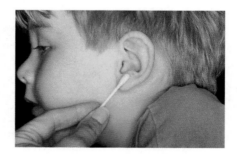

Cleaning Hands

It's important to make sure that your hands are clean. If you have been playing outside, or petting your dog or cat, you should wash your hands before eating anything. There are loads of germs on your hands and you don't want them in your mouth. So use soap and get your hands very sudsy to get them clean before you eat your sandwich for lunch.

It's also very important to wash your hands after going to the bathroom. Always use soap to make sure you are getting them clean.

Cleaning Your Face

If you have a dirty face, your friends might not want to play with you. So, washing your face can be fun – you can even put a bunch of suds on your chin so you look like you have a beard!

How fun is that?

Cleaning Your Toes

You probably don't think much about your feet and toes, but you should pay special attention to getting your toes clean. They can get dry and cracked if you don't take good care of them. Besides, who wants to have dirty feet?

You might be too big to sit on the sink like this little guy – but he has the right idea about cleaning his feet and toes.

Washing Your Hair

Your hair needs to be shampooed. Your parents can tell you how often to wash your hair, but most boys wash their hair every time they shower. If you have long hair, you might not want to wash it every day in the shower. But boys with short hair usually shampoo their hair every time.

You can even sing a song while you're in the shower! If you want to.

Dirty Feet

We've already talked about cleaning your hands, but think about your feet for a minute. You walk around outside barefoot or in flip flops and get so much dirt on them. And you carry this dirt around all day! When you get into bed, you don't want all this dirt on your clean sheets when you sleep – and you know that your mom and dad don't want you getting all this dirt in your bed either.

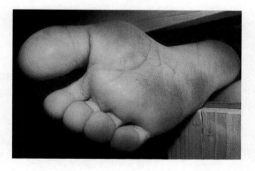

It's not easy for you to see the bottoms of your feet, but if you've been playing outside – they probably look like this. You should wash them before you get in bed.

Brushing Your Teeth

It's important to brush your teeth several times a day. This is the way to keep from having bad breath. No one likes to talk to people with bad breath. So be sure you use a toothbrush and toothpaste to keep your teeth and your mouth clean.

Don't Be Stinky

When you are dirty, you probably smell bad. The best way to keep from being stinky is to take care of your body by keeping it clean. The older you get, the more important it is to shower regularly.

You will feel great when you're clean.

So, suds up!

You may even feel like a superhero!

*For more Kids Picture Books Visit Lisa Strattin's
author page on amazon.com.*

*To see upcoming titles, visit my website at
LisaStrattin.com – all books available on kindle!*

**If you enjoyed this book, please stop by the
amazon.com page and leave a review.**

50176689R00018

Made in the USA
Lexington, KY
05 March 2016